CORAL'S & REEF'S OF THE SOUTH PACIFIC

Welcome to my book of Coral's and Reef's of the South Pacific,

Each and everyone of these fantastic pictures was captured by myself during my amazing travels through the south pacific Islands.

Pictures that are featured in this book come from the Islands of :

Lifou Island

Champagne Bay

Kiriwina Island

Conflict Island

Thank you for sharing my passion for the ocean and marine life.

Published By Z. R. Holden

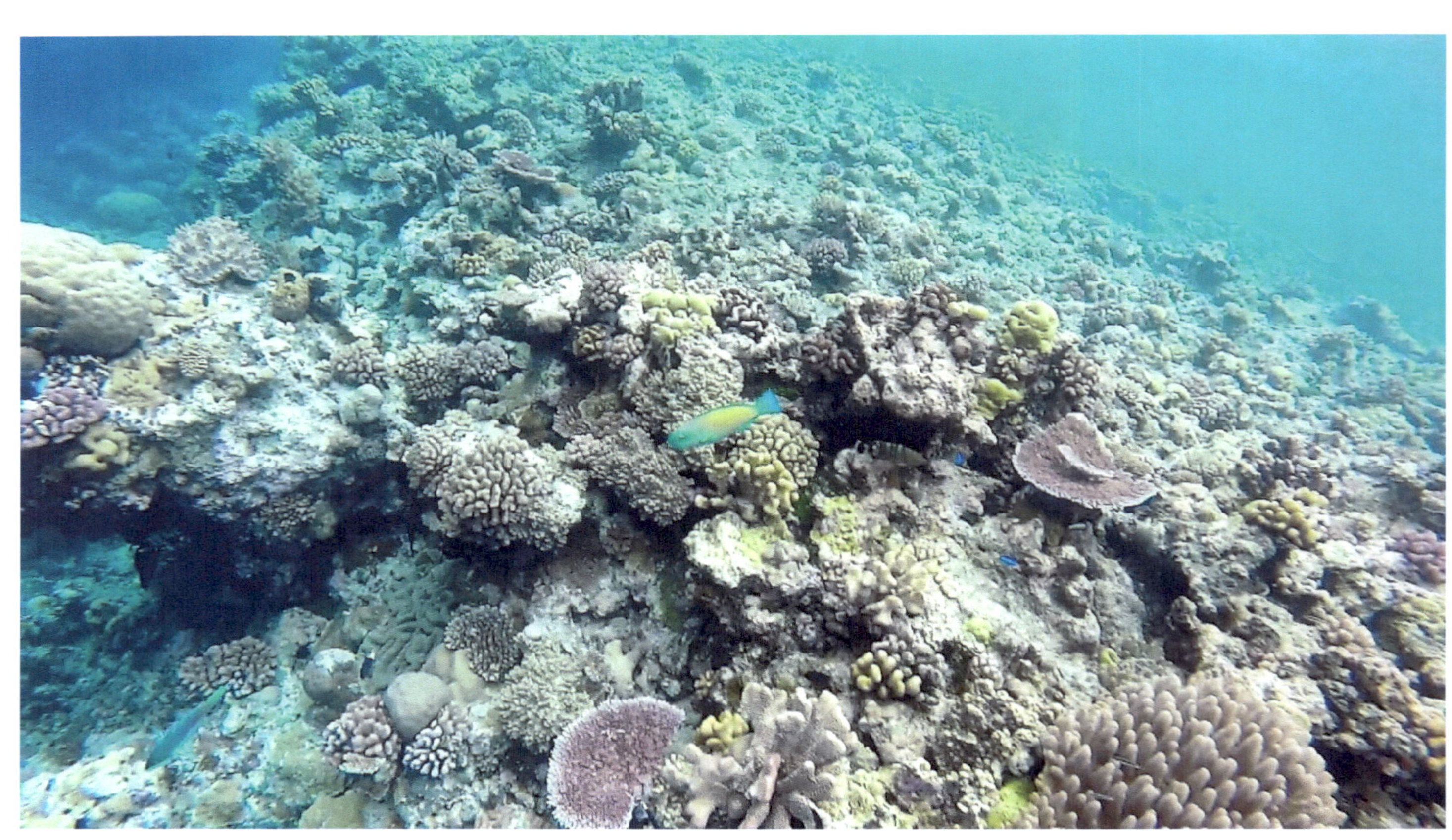